60030

The A-Z of Rock and Minerals

David Orme and Helen Bird

CW0054037

Contents

1

Introduction

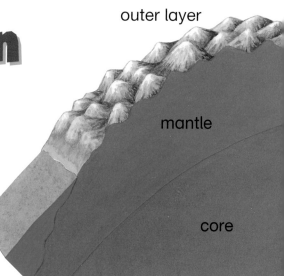

outer layer

mantle

core

The surface of the Earth is a hard crust made of rocks.

What is a rock?

A rock is a mix of minerals. If we look closely at a rock, or view it under a microscope, we can see the different minerals. The rock **granite** is made up of the mineral **quartz** and two or three other minerals.

Key:

Find out more about **words in bold** in the A–Z section of this book.

Find out more about *words in italic* in the Glossary.

Granite is made up of quartz, silica and other minerals.

Rocks are described by the size of the pieces of the minerals they contain. This is called the grain size. If the size of the grains is too small to be seen, the rock is described as fine. If the grain size is between 0.1 and 2 millimetres, the rock is medium. Rocks with larger grains are described as coarse.

A fine-grained rock

A coarse-grained rock

What is a mineral?

Minerals often look like rocks but are different because they always contain the same sort of substance. Minerals which have good *crystal* shapes and colours are sometimes called gemstones and are used to make jewellery.

Minerals are described by how hard they are. The softest mineral is called **talc** and has a hardness of 1. The hardest mineral is a **diamond** and has a hardness of 10.

What is a metal?

A metal is a mineral which has special properties in its pure form. Most metals are found as *ores*, which are rocks where the metal is chemically combined with other substances.

Some metals, such as **lead** or **copper**, are very soft and can easily be shaped into many different objects. Other metals, such as **gold** and **silver**, are very attractive as well as being quite soft. They are often used to make jewellery. Common metals such as aluminium (see **bauxite**) and **iron** are used to build many things from huge buildings to aeroplanes.

The London Eye is a huge metal structure.

amethyst

Amethyst is a *semiprecious* mineral which is often used in jewellery. It is usually found as purple *crystals*. Amethysts are found in Brazil, Canada and Uruguay.

a

basalt

Basalt is a rock with a very fine grain. It is usually black or dark grey. It can form as large blocks. Some places, like the Giant's Causeway in Ireland, have big areas of basalt. Most basalt is formed by **lava** flows.

b

The Giant's Causeway in Ireland has large blocks of basalt.

bauxite

Bauxite is a claylike rock. It is the main *ore* of the metal aluminium. It is very common and is found all around the world. The word comes from Les Baux in France where bauxite was first found.

calcite

Calcite is another quite soft mineral. It has a hardness of 3. It can be found as clear *crystals* in **limestone** and **marble**. It is the most important mineral in these rocks. Its crystal form is used in optical instruments. It is also used in the steel, chemical and glass industries.

chalk

Chalk is a fine-grained rock. It is a very pure form of **limestone**. **Fossils** of ancient sea creatures are often found in chalk.

The chalk cliffs of Dover in England look white.

coal

Coal is a rock formed from trees and plants that were buried in the earth millions of years ago. The weight of the earth above has compressed them into a hard, black material.

Coal is very useful because it burns with great heat. It can be used to heat houses or to make electricity. The substances in coal can be used to make a wide range of things, such as plastic.

copper

Copper is a metal and also a mineral. Its hardness is between $2\frac{1}{2}$ and 3 which means it is soft and can be made into objects quite easily. Water pipes are often made of copper, and it is also used for making jewellery and other objects. It is possible to find small amounts of pure copper in the form of *nuggets* but it is also found mixed with other minerals. These rocks are called copper *ores*. Copper is mined in Australia, Chile, Peru, Mexico, the United States of America and Central Africa.

d

diamond

Diamonds are the hardest minerals with a hardness of 10. Diamonds are usually found in **kimberlite** which is a rock found very deep in the earth. For this reason, most diamonds are mined. Many diamonds come from Africa: South Africa and Sierra Leone are important diamond-producing countries.

Sometimes diamonds are found in gravel near rivers and beaches. Clear, well-shaped diamonds are *precious* gems used in jewellery. They are also important for use in other ways because they are so hard. They are often used to make cutting tools, such as drill bits.

emerald

Emeralds are green *crystals* formed of a mineral called beryl. They are *precious* gems with a hardness of between $7\frac{1}{2}$ and 8. They are mostly used to make jewellery. Emeralds are found in the United States of America, Australia and Colombia.

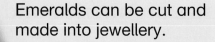

Emeralds can be cut and made into jewellery.

flint

Flint is a rock usually found in **limestone** and **chalk**. Lumps of flint are found coated in a **limestone** covering and embedded in the other rocks.

Flint is fine-grained and smooth, and is made of **silica**. When it is fresh it is nearly black. When it is broken it has very sharp edges.

In the *Stone Age*, flint was used to make tools, such as axes, knives and arrowheads.

These are arrowheads from India.

fossils

Fossils are remains of plants or animals preserved in rocks. Sometimes a fossil is a print in the rock. Sometimes parts of the plant or animal have changed into a mineral. These fossils still keep the shape of the plant, or of the bones or shell of the creature. Fossils are often found in **limestone** cliffs or in lumps of **coal**.

g

gold

Gold is a soft metal mineral. Its hardness is between $2\frac{1}{2}$ and 3. It is easy to recognize because of its colour. Sometimes it is found in a lump called a *nugget*. Tiny grains of gold can be carried long distances by streams. People try to collect gold from streams by *panning*. Most gold is mined. South Africa, Russia, the United States of America and Australia are important gold-producing countries.

Gold is valuable because of its beautiful colour and because it does not *corrode*. People have valued gold for many centuries and it is used to make jewellery and other objects of value. It was once even used as money.

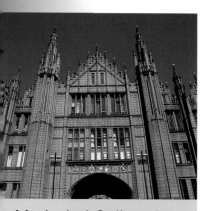

Marischal College is just one of Aberdeen's many granite buildings.

granite

This is a coarse-grained rock. Because it is quite hard, it is often used for building. Aberdeen in Scotland is called the Granite City because of the many granite buildings.

The mix of minerals in granite includes **quartz**. Granite is an *igneous rock*.

hematite

Hematite is a mineral found as an *ore* and is rich in **iron**. It is called an ore because the pure metal has combined with oxygen, but it is still a mineral because it is not combined with any other mineral. Its hardness is between 5 and 6. It is important because it is used as a source of iron.

This is an iron ore mine in Western Australia.

iron

Pure iron is a metal. Its hardness is $4\frac{1}{2}$. It is found in many rocks and minerals such as ironstone rocks and iron pyrites. Iron pyrites is sometimes called "fool's gold" because it is dark gold in colour and looks like metal *crystals*. **Meteorites** nearly always contain iron.

jade

Jade is a mineral used as a *semiprecious stone* and is often made into jewellery. Its hardness is 6, but it can be carved and made into all sorts of figures and shapes. In China, there are jade figures which date from Neolithic times (3000–1500 BC). Jade can be different colours, depending on which other minerals are mixed in with it. Pure jade is usually green. The finest jade comes from Burma.

This carved jade head is from China.

kimberlite

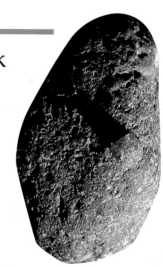

Kimberlite is a coarse-grained rock that is formed deep underground. It forces its way up to the surface in thin layers called *veins*. It is the main source of **diamonds**. Kimberlite is found in the diamond fields of South Africa.

lava

Lava is molten rock. This rock forms deep under the earth, where it is so hot that the rock is liquid. Molten lava and rocks are sometimes forced out of the earth by volcanoes.

When lava cools, it turns into a hard rock. The most common sort of this is called **basalt**. Rocks formed by heat under the earth are called *igneous rocks*.

lead

Lead is a very heavy, soft metal with a hardness of only 2. Lead does not *corrode* and, because it is very soft, it is easy to bend into different shapes. This makes it very useful. In the past it was used to make pipes, and thin sheets were sometimes used to make roofs. People try not to use lead today as it can often be poisonous. Lead is most often used today in big batteries such as the ones in cars. The main source of lead is an *ore* called galena.

limestone

Limestone is a rock that was formed over millions of years at the bottom of the sea from the shells of tiny sea creatures. Rocks formed in this way are called *sedimentary rocks*.

Limestone often contains **fossils**. It is regularly used in the building trade.

This carved church is made from limestone.

14

marble

Marble is a soft rock of medium to coarse grains found in Italy and India. It can be polished to give a very smooth surface and can easily be scratched with a knife. Marble is a *metamorphic rock*. The changes made in it by heat or pressure sometimes produce beautiful patterns. Marble is used for sculptures and to decorate buildings.

Marble statues are often found in stately homes and museums.

meteorites

Meteorites are rocks from space. Most are small and burn away completely in the air. Each year, about 500 meteorites are big enough to reach the ground. Many meteorites contain **iron**.

oil

Oil is a thick, sticky liquid containing a mixture of useful chemicals. It is a mineral formed from the bodies of tiny animals that sank to the bottom of the sea millions of years ago. There are large oil reserves in the Middle East, and in the shallow seas surrounding the continents. Some oil is *distilled* from a rock called oil shale.

A "nodding donkey" pumps oil from under the ground.

Liquid oil pumped from the rocks is called crude oil. Some crude oil will be turned into petrol, some into a wide range of things such as plastic and medicines – even perfume!

opal

Opal is a gemstone made mainly of **silica**. Opal is often found in areas of hot springs and *geysers*. Many opals are found in South Australia.

pitchblende

Pitchblende is a very heavy rock containing the *radioactive* minerals uranium and radium. These minerals are used in nuclear power stations, in nuclear weapons and in some special medical equipment. It is mined in Central Africa, Canada and the United States.

Pitchblende is used in nuclear power stations.

quartz

Quartz is a very common mineral made mainly of **silica**. Quartz can form beautiful *crystals* in a range of colours. Some are *semiprecious stones* such as **amethysts** and citrines. Rose quartz is pink. Quartz has a hardness of 7.

rock salt

Rock salt is another name for halite. This mineral is used to make table salt after the *impurities* have been removed. It can be obtained from the sea, but most salt comes from underground mines. There are large salt deposits in Poland and Russia.

17

ruby

Rubies are red *crystals* from the mineral corundum and have a hardness of 9. Blue crystals from the same mineral are called sapphires. Both rubies and sapphires are *precious* stones and are often used in jewellery. The finest rubies are found in Burma and Thailand.

silica

S

Silica is the Earth's most common mineral. It has many forms, such as **flint** and **quartz**. The sand you can see on the beach is mainly made of silica. Silica is used to make glass.

Granite contains silica.

silver

Silver is a beautiful metal, often used to make jewellery, tableware and ornaments. It is a soft metal with a hardness of 3, so it is often combined with other metals to make it harder. Most of the world's silver comes from South America.

Silver is a beautiful metal and ideal for moulding.

slate

Slate is a *metamorphic rock* that splits into thin sheets. These sheets are mainly used to make paving slabs or roofs for buildings. Slate is mined in the United States and Britain.

talc

Talc is the softest of all minerals with a hardness of 1. It is purified and powdered to make talcum powder. Some forms of talc are known as soapstone. This is easily carved to make ornaments. The Inuit people of Northern Canada, for example, use soapstone for their carvings of animals and people.

turquoise

Turquoise is a fine-grained, greenish-blue coloured *semiprecious stone*. It is often used for decoration by Native Americans in Colorado and New Mexico in the United States.

volcanic rocks

Volcanic rocks are formed from layers of ash built up during volcanic eruptions. The ash then cements together to form rock. When there are lots of eruptions, volcanic rocks can build up to form islands.
This is how the island of Surtsey near Iceland, for example, was formed.

As the volcano erupts, it produces huge ash clouds.

zircon

Zircon is a hard mineral found in *igneous rocks* such as **granite**. Some zircon *crystals* are used as gemstones. Zircons are found in many countries including Australia, Canada, Brazil and Sri Lanka. The metal zirconium is extracted from the *ore* zircon.

Glossary

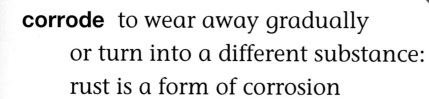

corrode to wear away gradually or turn into a different substance: rust is a form of corrosion

crystals minerals that have formed into regular shapes, sometimes transparent

distilled distillation is a method used to get a pure liquid from a mixture: the mixture is heated until the liquid boils and turns to gas; then the gas is collected and cooled quickly to turn it back to liquid

geysers hot springs that throw up fountains of very hot water from time to time

igneous rocks rocks produced from melted rocks that have hardened from deep in the earth

impurities unwanted chemicals

metamorphic rocks sedimentary rocks that have been changed by great heat or pressure

A geyser erupts under pressure sending tonnes of water into the air.

nugget mineral formed into a lump

ore rock containing a particular mineral

panning using a flat pan to extract gold from water flowing down a river

precious worth a lot of money: a precious stone, for example, is of great value

radioactive a radioactive substance gives off invisible rays: some of these are very useful, but they can also be dangerous

sedimentary rocks rocks formed by plants and animals laid down gradually at the bottom of the sea and rivers

semiprecious stones minerals, usually crystals, used to make jewellery but not as rare and valuable as precious gemstones such as diamonds or rubies

Stone Age the period in history before metal was used to make tools

veins minerals formed in long layers in the earth, like the veins of a person or animal